Answers to Questions Teachers Ask about Sensory Integration

(including Sensory Processing Disorder)

Forms, Checklists, and Practical Tools
for Teachers and Parents

Jane Koomar, PhD, OTR/L

Carol Kranowitz, MA

Stacey Szklut, MS, OTR/L

Lynn Balzer-Martin, PhD, OTR

Elizabeth Haber, MS, OTR/L

Deanna Iris Sava, MS, OTR/L

Sensory
RESURCES LLC
Las Vegas

Developed with OTA-Watertown
Watertown, MA

Printed in the United States

5th Printing—October 2005

2500 Chandler Ave., Ste. 3
Las Vegas, NV 89120-4064
Tel. 888-357-5867
Fax 702-891-8899
email: Orders@SensoryResources.com
www.SensoryResources.com

ISBN-13:   978-1-931615-03-7
ISBN-10:   1-931615-03-9

Contents

Introduction

Sensory processing disorder (sometimes called "dysfunction in sensory integration") is a "hidden tax" that may affect between 5% and 20% (depending on defining criteria) of the children in your class. As a teacher, you surely notice the out-of-sync behavior of certain children. Perhaps you wish to become more skillful in reaching and teaching these challenging students.

How can a teacher…

- Recognize Sensory Processing Disorder?

- Understand how Sensory Processing Disorder may interfere with a child's motor coordination, muscle tone, fine motor skills, visual perception, and relationships with others?

- Discern a child's unique pattern of out-of-sync behavior?

- Help a child recover after a "meltdown?"

- Develop strategies to prevent future meltdowns?

- Approach a child who is simultaneously oversensitive to one kind of stimulation and undersensitive to another kind?

- Help children identify their own needs for the right amount of sensory stimulation?

- Collaborate with parents, occupational therapists, and other professionals on a child's behalf?

- Provide a safe, appropriate, "sensory diet" in the classroom that will benefit all the students?

- Structure a calm and organized classroom?

- Manage his or her own behavior when a child "pushes those buttons?"

- Always, always remember that these are good children who are trying their best in a confusing world?

Answers to Questions Teachers Ask about Sensory Integration will answer these questions and many more.

Sincerely,

Carol Kranowitz

What Is Sensory Integration?

Every day, we receive a great deal of information from our senses. We use this information to organize our behavior and successfully interact in the world. Our senses give us information about the physical status of our body and the environment around us. Think of the senses: sight, hearing, touch, taste, and smell. Yet, there are many other sensations that are just as essential to survival. Our nervous system detects changes in movement and gravity. These sensory systems include: 1) balance and movement (our vestibular sense—the knowledge of the position of one's head in relation to gravity and movement, which is used to come down a slide or ride a playground swing without falling off), and 2) muscle and joint sense (proprioception—the internal awareness of the position of one's joints and muscles in space), which allows you to lift a spoon to your mouth without spilling your soup.

Our brains must organize this information so that we may function in everyday situations such as in the classroom, at home, on the playground, and during social interactions. When one reveals all of the sensory modalities, it is truly amazing that one brain can organize input from all senses simultaneously and still come up with a response to the demands of the environment. The complex nature of this interaction is reflected in the following example: Your teacher says, mother, or another adult says, "Johnny, please put on your coat." You respond by:

1) Focusing your attention on the person speaking and hearing what is said.

2) Screening out other information going on around you.

3) Seeing the coat and adequately making a plan for how to begin.

4) Seeing the armhole openings and sensing muscle and joint position, which allows you to know where to put your arms in relation to the coat sleeves.

5) With your sensitive touch awareness, feeling that the coat is on your body correctly.

6) Relying on adequate motor planning, touch awareness, and fine motor skills to enable you to zip or button your coat.

We could continue with this breakdown, but the point is that the central nervous system is constantly focusing, screening, sorting, and responding to sensory information, both from the external environment and internal receptors in order to perform purposeful activities. Imagine the amount of sensory integration needed to sit in a chair, pay attention in an active classroom, copy an assignment, or read a book.

Sensory Integration Disorders

What happens if one or more of our senses are not being interpreted properly? A child with vague or hazy feedback about his sense of touch, body position, or movement and gravity is in a world totally foreign to ours. Imagine yourself in a world where something as basic and reliable as the pull of gravity or other children's touch upon you is perceived as something unreliable, inconsistent, or threatening. You would not feel the usual security, safety, and fun that other children experience.

When the process of sensory integration is disordered, a number of problems in learning, motor development, or behavior may be observed:

Sensory problem	Signs or behavior
Overly sensitive to touch, movements, sights, or sounds	Behavior issues: distractible, withdrawing when touched, avoiding certain textures, clothes, foods. Fearful reaction to ordinary movement activities, like playground play. Sensitive to loud noises.
Under-reactive to sensory stimulation	Seeks out intense sensory experiences, such as body whirling, falling, and crashing into objects. May fluctuate between under- and over-responsiveness.
Unusually high/low activity level	Constantly on the move or may be slow to get going and then fatigue easily.
Coordination problems	Could have poor balance; have great difficulty learning a new task that requires motor coordination or appears awkward, stiff, or clumsy.
Delays in academic achievement or activities of daily living	May have problems in academic areas, despite normal or above intelligence. Could have problems with handwriting, using scissors, tying shoes, buttoning, and zipping clothes.
Poor organization of behavior	May be impulsive or distractible, show lack of planning in approach to tasks, or not anticipate result of actions. May have difficulty adjusting to a new situation or following directions. May get frustrated, aggressive, or withdrawn when encountering failure.
Poor self-concept	Could appear lazy, bored, or unmotivated. May avoid tasks and appear stubborn or troublesome.

Sensory Integration Treatment

Occupational therapy with training in sensory integration provides therapeutic activities to facilitate child-directed treatment sessions. The child with sensory integrative dysfunction may participate in play activities, but he does not play in a manner that is integrated or organized.

The child needs an environment with suspended equipment specially designed to meet his needs. The therapist designs an environment to enable the child to interact more effectively. Following diagnosis of the child's sensory system, the therapist encourages and assists the child in choosing activities that provide the appropriate amount of sensory input.

The therapist tries to carefully balance structure and freedom in a way that leads to constructive exploration. This balance is not easily achieved. Free play does not inevitably, in itself, further sensory integration. If it did, many children with dysfunction would have solved their own problems. But too much structure does not allow growth.

By balancing structure and freedom, the therapist helps the child to develop both his neural organization and his inner direction. The child is given as much control over therapy as he can handle, as long as his activity is therapeutic. The therapist controls the environment while the child controls his own actions.

Self-confidence, or an improved attitude about one's self, is often the first change parents notice in their children after they have started therapy. The child becomes more in command of his life because he develops better control of his body as his nervous system functions better.

Occupational Therapy Associates - Watertown, P.C.

Executive Director
Jane Koomar, Ph.D., OTR/L, FAOTA
Clinical Director
Stacey Szklut, M.S., OTR/L

124 Watertown St.
Watertown, MA 02472

Phone 617-923-4410
Fax 617-923-0468
Email: OTAWater@aol.com

What Is Occupational Therapy?

There are many definitions of occupational therapy. Here are a few of them:

Occupational therapy involves the "therapeutic use of work, self-care, and play activities to increase independent function, enhance development, and prevent disability. It may include adaptation of task or environment to achieve maximum independence and to enhance the quality of life." Official definition of occupational therapy as passed by the American Occupational Therapy Association Executive Board, 1976.

"Occupational therapy is the use of purposeful activity or interventions designed to achieve functional outcomes which promote health, prevent injury or disability, and which develop, improve, sustain or restore the highest possible level of independence of any individual who has an injury, illness, cognitive impairment, psychosocial dysfunction, mental illness, developmental or learning disability, or other disorders or conditions. It includes assessment by means of skilled observation or evaluation through the administration and interpretation of standardized or nonstandardized tests and measurements." Definition of Occupational Therapy Practice for State Regulation by the American Occupational Therapy Association, 1994.

"Occupational therapy helps children and young adults with disabilities from birth to 21 years of age to benefit from their educational programs. We focus on the student's performance in the areas of hand skills, eating, self-care, social skills, and play/leisure skills. Services may include assessment to determine strength/needs; collaborating with teachers, families, students, and others on environmental and material adaptations; developing strategies and activities to enhance performance; and providing student specific interventions." School System Special Interest Section.

"Occupational therapy is a health profession which uses therapeutic purposeful activities to help children and adults function better physically, emotionally, academically, and socially in their daily activities." "Occupational Therapy and the School-Aged Child: A reference guide for parents and teachers" by the Easter Seal Rehabilitation Center of Will-Grundy Counties, Joliet, IL.

Registered occupational therapists (OTRs) often work in collaboration with certified occupational therapist assistants (COTAs). The following paragraphs help the reader understand the important role played by COTAs.

Certified occupational therapist assistants (COTAs) assist with the evaluation and treatment of individuals with injuries, cognitive impairments, psychosocial dysfunctions, mental illness, developmental or learning disabilities, physical disabilities, or other disorders or conditions.

Under the supervision of occupational therapists (OTs), COTAs:

(1) contribute to the evaluation process through the administration of assessments (standardized and non-standardized) for which they have established competency; and

(2) implement therapeutic interventions that use purposeful activity for developing, improving, sustaining or restoring function in performance skills and leisure capacities.

The performance components (sensorimotor, cognitive, psychosocial, and psychological) are the elements of performance in which COTAs intervene for the purpose of attaining an individual's highest level of functional independence within the appropriate environmental context.

Under the supervision of an OT, COTAs also assist in the design, development, adaptation, application or training in the use of assistive technology devices; the design, fabrication or application of orthotic devices; training in the use of orthotic or prosthetic devices; application of physical agent modalities; and the adaptation of environments and processes to enhance functional performance.

How to Get the Most Out of *Answers to Questions Teachers Ask...*

User support and appreciation of more useful and practical information on sensory integration has been very encouraging to us. We'll continue to make helpful resource information available to teachers and other school professionals. Creating a common baseline for understanding sensory processing challenges is our passion and goal.

We would like to share with you what we see as the various uses for *Answers to Questions Teachers Ask About Sensory Integration*. This booklet contains numerous, reproducible checklists and charts. Use the checklists to acquaint yourself with some of the "red flags" to watch out for when trying to detect sensory processing problems.

If you have concerns about a particular student, you may want to make a copy of the checklist appropriate for his or her age and see if a significant pattern of responses emerge. Asking a fellow teacher or school professional to fill out another copy of the checklist can broaden your understanding of the child.

Please share this resource and information. As therapists working for years in medical and educational settings, we know that school professionals will network helpful information if it is presented in a competent and accessible manner.

A teacher we know was a little apprehensive that she didn't have the training or background to work effectively with three of her students in her classroom of twenty-nine. She combed through the resource section of Carol Stock Kranowitz' book *The Out-of-Sync Child*, (we highly recommend this book to anyone interacting regularly with a special needs child) highlighting all the organizations she wanted to learn more about.

Then she wrote a generic "request for information" letter and mailed copies to over thirty organizations. We got to know her because she contacted us via that method! We encourage you to use the resource lists provided here in a similar way.

Teachers of children ages eight or older, please embrace the lists and exercises with a mind for how they can be applied to older kids. Children (and adults) learn subtle ways to mask sensory defensive behaviors, a tendency that can have severe social consequences as they get older.

An observant teacher can learn the fundamentals and modify them to fit the cognitive level of the older child. School administrators, school psychologists, and other school personnel faced with the challenge of providing effective service for children with learning disabilities will benefit from the broader sense of understanding they will get from the information presented in this booklet.

Parents who desire better working relationships with school personnel can give this product to the school. Sharing the information with classroom teachers, paraprofessionals, physical education teachers, and music and art teachers is a great way to help them understand and accommodate the child's special needs.

We are sincerely glad that you have found your way into the domain of information available on sensory processing disorders. May you soak up the information as it was intended to be enjoyed; with pauses for summary, reflection and true learning.

Comparison of Typical Sensory Processing & Sensory Processing Disorder

	Typical Sensory Processing	Sensory Processing Disorder
What:	The ability to take in sensory information from one's body and the environment, to organize this information, and to use it to function in daily life.	The ineffective processing of tactile, vestibular, and/or proprioceptive sensations. The person may have difficulty with other basic senses, too.
Where:	Occurs in the central nervous system (nerves, spinal cord, and brain), in a well balanced, reciprocal process.	Occurs in the central nervous system, where the flow between sensory input and motor output is disrupted.
Why:	To enable a person to survive, to make sense of the world, and to interact with the environment in meaningful ways.	Neuronal connections in the central nervous system are ineffective.
How:	Happens automatically as the person takes in sensations through sensory receptors in the skin, the inner ear, the muscles, and the eyes, ears, mouth and nose.	Sensory neurons do not send effective messages into the central nervous system, and/or motor neurons do not send effective messages out to the body for adaptive behavioral responses.
When:	Begins in utero and continues developing throughout childhood, with most functions established by adolescence.	Occurs before, during, or shortly after birth.

Adapted from: *The Out-of-Sync Child,* 2nd ed. © 2005 Carol S. Kranowitz. All rights reserved.

Organizing Sensory Input and Activities for the Classroom

How a child's environment and day-to-day activities are presented can have a massive impact on his or her responsiveness to life. We found the Occupational Therapy Associates - Watertown, P.C.'s summary, presented below, very helpful in developing more effective and nurturing environments, both in the classroom and at home.

Environment:

Children with sensory integration difficulties can easily become overwhelmed by extraneous visual and auditory input. By controlling the classroom environment, you can maximize children's ability to remain focused and organized.

- As much as possible, limit the amount of extraneous visual material you have hanging from the ceiling and on the walls.

- Store fine motor and math manipulatives inside plastic containers or cubbies.

- Be sure that all materials have an organized and labeled place where they belong. Help desk organization with a picture template of where each item belongs inside the desk.

- Tape a number or letter line directly on the child's desk if she gets distracted when using the one on the blackboard or wall. Also, tape spelling words to the desk rather than to the blackboard, if necessary.

- Limit extraneous auditory input from the hallway by closing your classroom door. Seat the child who has sensory sensitivities and distractibility away from open windows and doors.

- If the loud speaker in your room has static or is very loud when announcements are made, remove the cover and line it with an old tee shirt or newspaper. This will reduce the loud "surprise" factor.

- As much as possible, prepare the child who is sensitive to noise for clean-up bells, fire drills, and morning announcements.

Schedule:

Children with sensory integration difficulties will benefit from a predictable schedule.

- Each morning, outline the schedule for the day with the class. Highlight any changes from the typical routine that will occur that day.

- Discuss or create a "story" about unexpected events before they occur (e.g., fire drills or assemblies) to help children prepare for these potentially overwhelming situations.

- Help younger children make transitions between activities by creating a "clean-up" song or "new game" song.

- Assist older children in keeping a homework organizer for their schedule and homework assignments. Check this after each class to make sure the homework assignments are correct and the child understands what the homework entails.

- Color-code notebooks and book covers to assist the child in having the correct materials for each class (e.g., red for math, blue for science).

General Organizing Sensory Activities:

The types of sensory input that are "organizing" include pressure, rhythm, oral-motor input, and exercise.

- Placing your hands on the child's shoulders or head with safe, firm pressure can help him slow down.

- Create a quiet corner in the room (e.g., a well-ventilated refrigerator box "house," reading center, listening center with headphones, and music or books on tape).

- During times of independent work, try playing classical music in the background. Mozart and Vivaldi are thought to be conducive to learning.

- Teach kids to take several breaths before making a transition to a busy environment or working on a difficult project.

- Have younger children "march" from one activity to another. The rhythmical body motion and input to the feet can be organizing.

- Input to the mouth through drinking or eating chewy or crunchy foods helps with focus and organization. Allow children to have water bottles or crunchy snacks at their desks as needed.

- Have younger children try to "hold the walls up" or "push the walls down" while waiting in line at the bathroom, etc. Teach older children to do pushups in their seats with their hands.

- People often "fiddle" with small objects such as erasers or paper clips as a way to maintain attention. If it is not interfering with classroom learning and is safe for the child and circumstance, allow "fiddle" objects during listening activities.

- Take "movement breaks" to stand up and stretch between classroom activities.

Occupational Therapy Associates - Watertown, P.C.

Executive Director
Jane Koomar, Ph.D., OTR/L, FAOTA
Clinical Director
Stacey Szklut, M.S., OTR/L

124 Watertown St.
Watertown, MA 02472

Phone 617-923-4410
Fax 617-923-0468
Email: OTAWater@aol.com

Classroom Accommodation Checklist

The Classroom Accommodation Checklist, also provided by the Occupational Therapy Association - Watertown, P.C., is geared toward providing the child with effective and regulated stimulus that will help facilitate sensory integration. It explores in more depth the physical elements of sensory input. Read through the suggestions and check off those you find applicable to a particular child. Share the list with parents and other teachers as a way to enhance communication and understanding among all the folks helping a child on his or her journey.

Child's Name: _____ Date: _____

Sensory Processing:

At each moment a person takes in information from the environment and his or her body and must screen what is important to organize him/herself to act on the environment.

☐ For the student who becomes over-stimulated by the environment, provide quiet, "time out" spaces to help the child regroup and become organized (e.g., a reading corner behind a bookshelf, under a table with pillows or bean bag chair in a quiet corner).

☐ For the student who experiences sensitivity to touch (tactile defensiveness), allow the child to stand at the end of the line and arrange the classroom seating to minimize the risk of being jostled or bumped by classmates (i.e., have the child's desk either near the teacher or at the back of the room).

☐ When planning an art activity, modifications to the activity may need to be made to accommodate the child who is sensitive to touch. (Be aware that materials such as glue, finger paints, clay, paper maché, etc. may cause the child to have an aversive response.) Using tools (i.e., hammer, paint brush, etc.) may help child participate more fully.

☐ Forewarn the child of any loud noises before they occur (e.g., bells or alarms).

☐ To minimize auditory distractions, a classroom with a rug or carpet would help decrease extraneous noises.

☐ To decrease fidgeting at the desk and promote improved postural adjustments, allow the student to stand at the desk or to work on the floor in a prone-on-elbows position (on stomach). A bungee cord or Thera-Band® wrapped around chair legs provides sensory input to assist child in remaining seated longer.

☐ Using a partially inflated air pillow (stadium seat) may help increase postural control by increasing sensory feedback in sitting.

☐ Allow the child to become a teacher's assistant and pass out papers so he is able to walk around the room appropriately with a goal-directed task.

☐ To increase postural muscle strength and endurance: swinging, jungle gyms, rope-climbing, calisthenics, pulling/pushing a wagon, carrying weighted objects, scooter boards in prone lying positions, and wheelbarrow walking are fine!

☐ Adjust the chair and table to a height suitable for the student to best perform table top work. (Feet touching the floor and the table height so the child's elbows can rest comfortably on top without hunched shoulders.)

☐ Children with low oral and postural tone often gain more control for fine motor tasks when given gum to chew on or hard candy to suck during writing activities. Use as permitted in the school setting.

☐ For children with oral motor control difficulties, modifications to the snack menu may need to be made to accommodate to the child's needs. Also, the child's sitting posture needs to be evaluated to determine if it has a direct effect on the child's difficulties with oral motor control. Please ask an occupational therapist for assistance in assessing these areas.

☐ Have the child with oral motor difficulties play with whistles, bubbles, or make pictures by blowing paint through straws (e.g., "Fire Works").

Fine Motor Skills:

Development of fine motor skills facilitates skills such as manipulating fasteners, writing, and scissor skills.

☐ Working on a vertical surface helps the child develop strength in his shoulder and wrist muscles, which are needed for writing. This can be done by writing on a blackboard, easel, desk easel or paper taped on the wall.

☐ To facilitate the development of the skill fingers (thumb, index, and middle fingers) that are necessary for the refinement of handwriting and scissor skills, the following activities are suggested: using a spray bottle to squirt water onto a picture, using tweezers to pick up cotton balls or other collage materials to make a picture, using small manipulatives such as buttons, beads, and "unfix" cubes.

☐ For the development of the child's web space (the "circle" that forms with the index finger and thumb) that is needed to hold a pencil correctly, the following activities are suggested: popping the plastic "bubbles" on packing sheets, opening/closing ziplock bags, snapping, winding up wind-up toys that have a knob, using an eyedropper to make pictures by mixing food coloring with water and dripping it onto paper towels, using tweezers to pick up small objects, spinning tops, using large plastic needles to sew yarn into pieces of burlap, and/or rolling balls of tissue paper to make pictures.

☐ To increase finger strength/control, use a hole punch, push pegs into clay, cut cardboard, and/or pick up small objects with tweezers.

☐ Provide activities to develop fine motor control and planning. Use games that involve spatial construction such as Legos,® Tinkertoys,® origami, woodworking, etc.

☐ Use Fiskar/Loop scissors as a precursor to regular scissor use. Practice scissor skills by cutting strips of paper, straws, and/or rolls of Play-Doh.®

☐ Check the child's scissor grasp (thumb and middle finger through the holes, the index finger stabilizes under the middle finger side for increased control) and remind the child to "steer" the paper with the non-preferred hand.

☐ Use of a molded pencil grip will provide a larger surface for grasp to improve written refinement (i.e., large markers, primary pencils, DLM grips, Stetro grips, bulb grips and "the pencil grip").

☐ Use activities that involve tactile/kinesthetic awareness to reinforce writing skills such as drawing large letters in the air or on a chalkboard, writing in Play-Doh or shaving cream, or practicing writing with eyes closed. Teach or review letter formation, beginning large and gradually reducing size.

☐ Provide primary lined paper or draw dotted guidelines on lined paper to help with spacing. Older students can be reminded to draw in their own guideline with a ruler.

☐ Remind child to use non-preferred hand or provide clipboard to stabilize paper.

☐ Practice visual-motor skills by drawing with shapes and letters. Ed Emberly has some great drawing books with wonderful ideas. These may be in your library! Make sample drawings larger if necessary and provide step-by-step instruction.

Motor Planning and Organizational Strategies:

Motor Planning is the ability to organize and sequence novel activities and affects the child's independence in self-help skills and motor development.

© 1999 Occupational Therapy Associates Watertown, P.C.

☐ For the student with difficulty in motor planning, give simple step-by-step directions. Help the child identify the steps needed to accomplish the task. Demonstrate or ask another student to model the motor activity, then ask the child to try.

☐ Use a consistent approach to teaching the child a new skill. Allow time for practice. It may take a child with motor planning delays much more time to "polish" a new skill.

☐ Present directions for new activities in child's best modality: visual, auditory, or multi-sensory to facilitate learning. Use modeling, demonstration and repetition as necessary. Monitor the child to be sure the information is understood and the task initiated.

☐ Help the student plan out a task by asking questions such as "What materials do you need?" "What do you do first?"

☐ For the child who has difficulty formulating ideas for projects or assignments, provide several suggestions or create a brainstorming session among a peer group.

☐ Set up any variety of activities in an obstacle course. Begin simply and increase the complexity as the student is able to handle the tasks. Also, "Simon Says" or sequencing games are great for motor planning.

☐ A child with motor planning difficulties may need assistance to recognize and improve on performance/work that is not accurate.

☐ To prepare the child for transitions, use a timer or warn ahead of time to identify when it is time to change activities.

☐ Using pictures or a list written on the blackboard to order the day's activities will help the child with sequencing difficulties organize the day for smoother transitions.

☐ Help the child develop organizational skills by having a consistent place to store materials once he/she has completed a task.

☐ To help the student stay organized and focused on challenging academic work, you can have the child use a finger or file card under a line to keep place in reading or math, use graph paper for math work, keep the amount of visual information presented on a page to a minimum, or cover an area of the page to expose one or two problems at a time.

☐ To provide additional structure, give the student letter and number guides to copy from. Tape to child's desk if needed.

☐ Allow extra time for written work until the child's writing skills improve and/or decrease the amount of written work in the classroom and at home as needed.

☐ Explore alternatives to the laborious effort of handwriting. Try using oral reporting, tape recorders, and multiple choice responses.

☐ Supplement handwriting with other methods of written expression (e.g., typing or keyboarding on a computer). Computer games or drawing programs are a good way to begin teaching computer keyboard skills.

Compiled by Trecker, Szklut, Gurney, and OTA Staff

Executive Director
Jane Koomar, Ph.D., OTR/L, FAOTA
Clinical Director
Stacey Szklut, M.S., OTR/L

124 Watertown St.
Watertown, MA 02472

Phone 617-923-4410
Fax 617-923-0468
Email: OTAWater@aol.com

Occupational Therapy Associates -
Watertown, P.C.

Infants and Toddlers Checklist (Birth to Age Two)

The following checklist, provided by the Occupational Therapy Associates—Watertown, P.C., will provide you with a very detailed evaluation of sensory integration issues. If the child demonstrates behaviors associated with sensory integration dysfunction (DSI), it may be necessary to seek further information through evaluation by a qualified occupational or physical therapist.

Child's Name: _____ Date: _____

Check areas of difficulty: underline specific problems and star (*) prominent difficulties. If child has overall difficulty in one category or shows several items in three or more categories, this may indicate a need for an occupational therapist evaluation.

Does the child exhibit the following behaviors?	Yes, frequently	Sometimes	Never	Comments
Dressing, Bathing, Touch				
1. Distressed when diapered or when diaper needs changing.				
2. Prefers certain clothing, complains that certain garments are too tight or itchy (for infants over 15 months).				
3. Distressed by having hair or face washed, or bathing.				
4. Distressed when clothes removed.				
5. Resists cuddling, pulls away or arches.				
6. Doesn't notice pain when falling, bumping, or when the doctor gives shots.				
7. Dislikes messy play.				
Movement				
1. In constant motion, rocking, running about, unable to sit still for an activity.				
2. Absent or brief crawling before walking (over 1 year).				
3. Distressed by being swung in air, swings, merry-go-rounds, car rides.				
4. Craves swinging and moving upside down.				
5. Clumsy, falling, poor balance, bumps into things (over 1 year).				
6. Fearful or hesitancy moving over changing surfaces (e.g., sidewalk to grass, carpet to wood floor).				

©1999 Occupational Therapy Associates Watertown, P.C.

Does the child exhibit the following behaviors?	Yes, frequently	Sometimes	Never	Comments
Listening, Language, and Sound				
1. Distressed by common sounds (e.g., music, singing, vacuuming, flushing toilet, raised voices).				
2. Doesn't respond to verbal cues (hearing not a problem over 1 year).				
3. None or very little vocalizing or babbling.				
4. Distracted by sounds not normally noticed by average person (e.g., furnace. refrigerator).				
Looking and Sight				
1.Sensitive to bright lights, cries or closes eyes.				
2.Avoids eye contact, turns away from the human face.				
3. Becomes overly excited or falls asleep in crowded, bustling settings such as a crowded supermarket, restaurant (over 1 year).				
4.Cannot pay attention with more than one toy or food item in view.				
Play Abilities				
1. Does not show ability for imitative play (older than 10 months).				
2. Wanders around aimlessly without focused exploration or purposeful play (over 15 months).				
3. Easily breaks toys and other things destructively (over 15 months).				
4. Needs total control of the environment ("runs the show").				
5. Amuses self appropriately for brief periods of time.				
6. Engages in repetitive play for long periods of time.				

Does the child exhibit the following behaviors?	Yes, frequently	Sometimes	Never	Comments
Emotional Attachment/ Emotional Functioning				
1. Prefers to play more with objects and toys than with people.				
2. Does not interact reciprocally (back and forth exchanges with caregiver).				
3. Hurts self or others (e.g., head banging, biting, or pinching).				
4. Everyone has difficulty understanding the child's cues or emotions.				
5. Does not seek connection with familiar persons.				
Self-Regulation				
1. Excessively irritable, fussy, colicky				
2. Can't calm self effectively by sucking on pacifier, looking at toys, or listening to caregiver (10 months and older).				
3. Can't change from one activity to another or from sleeping to awake without distress.				
4. Must be prepared in advance several times before change is introduced.				
Attention				
1. Easily distractible, fleeting attention				
2. Over focuses on one activity (e.g., TV, trains, wheels).				
3. Too distracted to stay seated for meals.				

Does the child exhibit the following behaviors?	Yes, frequently	Sometimes	Never	Comments
Eating, Sleeping				
1. Requires extensive help to fall asleep or wake up. Specify: rocking, long walking, stroking hair or back, car ride.				
2. Extreme food preferences for extended time periods.				
3. Excessive drooling beyond teething stage.				
4. Difficulty with sucking, chewing, or swallowing.				

How concerned are you about the above checked problems?   Not concerned   Slightly   Moderately   Very

Questions/Comments:

Child's Name: _____ Birth Date: _____ Age: _____

Date Completed: _____ Parents' Name(s): _____ Phone: _____

Name of Case Manager/Therapist/Teacher: _____

Name of Early Intervention/Preschool: _____

©1999 Occupational Therapy Associates Watertown, P.C.

Executive Director
Jane Koomar, Ph.D., OTR/L, FAOTA
Clinical Director
Stacey Szklut, M.S., OTR/L

124 Watertown St.
Watertown, MA 02472

Phone 617-923-4410
Fax 617-923-0468
Email: OTAWater@aol.com

Occupational Therapy Associates -
Watertown, P.C.

Preschool Checklist (Age Three to Four)

The following checklist provided by the Occupational Therapy Associates—Watertown, P.C. will provide you with a very detailed evaluation of sensory integration issues. If the child demonstrates behaviors associated with sensory integration dysfunction (DSI), it may be necessary to seek further information through evaluation by a qualified occupational or physical therapist.

Child's Name: _____ Date: _____

Check areas of difficulty: underline specific problems and star (*) prominent difficulties. If child has overall difficulty in one category or shows several items in three or more categories, this may indicate a need for an occupational therapist evaluation.

Does the child exhibit the following behaviors?	Yes, frequently	Sometimes	Never	Comments
Motor Skills				
1. Difficulty riding a riding toy, with feet pushing or propelling.				
2. Difficulty or hesitancy in climbing up and/or down stairs alternating feet.				
3. Dislikes playing with puzzles.				
4 Dislikes or avoids coloring or drawing.				
5. Dislikes playing with small manipulative toys (e.g., Duplos,® beads, or blocks).				
6. Difficulty with the use of a spoon or cup.				
7. Has very messy eating habits.				
8 Seems weaker or tires more easily than other children his age.				
9. Appears stiff, awkward, or clumsy in movement.				
10. Difficulty learning new motor tasks.				
11. Has difficulty getting on coat with zipper or putting on shoes (not tying).				
12. Uses too much force when playing with toys or interacting with children or pets.				
13. Walks on toes, now, or in the past.				

©1999 Occupational Therapy Associates Watertown, P.C.

Does the child exhibit the following behaviors?	Yes, frequently	Sometimes	Never	Comments
Movement and Balance				
1. Child appears to be in constant motion, unable to sit still for an activity.				
2. Appears fearful of going downstairs.				
3. Gets nauseated or vomits from other movement experiences, e.g., swings, playground merry-go-rounds.				
4. Seeks quantities of twirling or spinning.				
5. Needs quantities of stimulation on amusement park rides and swings.				
6. Hesitates to climb or play on playground equipment.				
7. Has trouble or hesitancy in learning to catch a ball.				
8. Dislikes active running games; (e.g., tag).				
9. Rocks himself/herself or bangs head when stressed.				
10. Seems to fall frequently.				
11. Has poor safety awareness when moving through space.				
12. Fearful of going down sliding board or on a swing.				

Does the child exhibit the following behaviors?	Yes, frequently	Sometimes	Never	Comments
Touch				
1. Seems unaware of being touched or bumped.				
2. Seems overly sensitive to being touched, pulls away from light touch.				
3. Has trouble remaining in busy or group situations (e.g., circle time, recess).				
4. Complains that clothing is uncomfortable and/or bothered by the tags in the back of shirts.				
5. Resists wearing short-sleeved shirts or short pants.				
6. Continues to examine objects by putting in the mouth (past age of 18 months).				
7. Dislikes being cuddled/hugged unless on child's terms.				
8. Seeks quantities of jumping and crashing.				
9. Avoids putting hands in messy substances (e.g., Play-Doh,® finger paint, glue).				
10. Is a picky eater, refuses many foods.				
11. Pinches, bites, or otherwise hurts self.				
12. Often unaware of bruises and cuts until someone calls it to his or her attention.				
13. Seems overly sensitive to slight bumps or scrapes.				
14. Tends to touch things constantly.				
15. Frequently pushes or hits other children.				

Does the child exhibit the following behaviors?	Yes, frequently	Sometimes	Never	Comments
Auditory/Language				
1. Has or has had repeated ear infections.				
2. Particularly distracted by sounds, seeming to hear sounds that go unnoticed by others.				
3. Doesn't respond consistently to verbal cues.				
4. Is overly sensitive to mildly loud noises (e.g., bells, toilet flush).				
5. Is hard to understand when she/he speaks.				
6. Has trouble following 1-2 step commands.				
7. History of delayed speech development.				
Bowel and Bladder				
1. Late in achieving bowel and bladder control.				
2. Occasionally has accidents during the day.				
3. If accidents occur, child does not seem to be aware ahead of time that elimination is about to occur.				
Emotional				
1. Does not accept changes in routine easily.				
2. Becomes easily frustrated.				
3. Apt to be impulsive, heedless, accident-prone.				
4. Has frequent outbursts or tantrums				
5. Tends to withdraw from groups; plays on the outskirts.				
6. Has trouble making needs known in appropriate manner.				
7. Avoids eye contact.				

©1999 Occupational Therapy Associates Watertown, P.C.

How concerned are you about the above checked problems?   Not concerned   Slightly   Moderately   Very

Questions/Comments:

Child's Name: _____ Birth Date: _____ Age: _____

Date Completed: _____ Parents' Name(s): _____ Phone: _____

Name of Case Manager/Therapist/Teacher: _____

Name of Early Intervention/Preschool: _____

Occupational Therapy Associates -
Watertown, P.C.

Executive Director
Jane Koomar, Ph.D., OTR/L, FAOTA
Clinical Director
Stacey Szklut, M.S., OTR/L

124 Watertown St.
Watertown, MA 02472

Phone 617-923-4410
Fax 617-923-0468
Email: OTAWater@aol.com

Answers to Questions Teachers Ask About Sensory Integration

School-Age Checklist (Age Five to Twelve)

The following checklist provided by the Occupational Therapy Associates—Watertown, P.C. will provide you with a very detailed evaluation of sensory integration issues. If the child demonstrates behaviors associated with sensory integration dysfunction (DSI), it may be necessary to seek further information through evaluation by a qualified occupational or physical therapist.

Child's Name: _____ Date: _____

Check areas of difficulty: underline specific problems and star (*) prominent difficulties. If child has overall difficulty in one category or shows several items in three or more categories, this may indicate a need for an occupational therapist evaluation.

Does the child exhibit the following behaviors?	Yes, frequently	Sometimes	Never	Comments
Gross Motor Skills				
1. Seems weaker or tires more easily than other children his/her age.				
2. Difficulty with hopping, jumping, skipping, or running compared to others his/her age.				
3. Appears stiff and awkward in movements.				
4. Clumsy or seems not to know how to move body; bumps into things.				
5. Tendency to confuse right and left body sides.				
6. Hesitates to climb or play on playground equipment.				
7. Reluctant to participate in sports or physical activity; prefers table activities.				
8. Seems to have difficulty learning new motor tasks.				
9. Difficulty pumping self on swing; poor skills in rhythmic clapping games.				
Fine Motor Skills				
1. Poor desk posture (slumps, leans on arm, head too close to work, other hand does not assist).				
2. Difficulty drawing, coloring, copying, cutting—avoidance of these activities.				
3. Poor pencil grasp; drops pencil frequently.				
4. Pencil lines are tight, wobbly, too faint or too dark; breaks pencil more often than usual.				
5. Tight pencil grasp: fatigues quickly in writing or other pencil and paper tasks.				
6. Hand dominance not well established (after age six).				
7. Difficulty in dressing; clothing off or on, buttons, zippers, tying bows on shoes.				

Does the child exhibit the following behaviors?	Yes, frequently	Sometimes	Never	Comments
Touch				
1. Seems overly sensitive to being touched; pulls away from light touch.				
3. Has trouble keeping hands to self, will poke or push other children.				
4. Touches things constantly; "learns" through his/her fingers.				
5. Has trouble controlling his interactions in group games such as tag, dodge ball.				
6. Avoids putting hands in messy substances (clay, finger paint, paste).				
7. Seem to be unaware of being touched or bumped.				
8. Has trouble remaining in busy or group situations; e.g., cafeteria, circle time.				
Movement and Balance				
1. Fearful moving through space (teeter-totter, swing.)				
2. Avoids activities that challenge balance; poor balance in motor activities.				
3. Seeks quantities of movement including swinging, spinning, bouncing, and jumping.				
4. Difficulty or hesitance learning to climb or descend stairs.				
5, Seems to fall frequently.				
6. Gets nauseated or vomits from other movement experiences; e.g., swings, playground merry-go-rounds.				
7. Appears to be in constant motion, unable to sit still for an activity.				
Visual Perception				
1. Difficulty naming or matching colors, shapes, or sizes.				
2. Difficulty in completing puzzles; trial and error placement of pieces.				
3. Reversals in words or letters after first grade.				
4. Difficulty coordinating eyes for following a moving object; keeping place in reading; copying from blackboard to desk.				

©1999 Occupational Therapy Associates Watertown, P.C.

Does the child exhibit the following behaviors?	Yes, frequently	Sometimes	Never	Comments
Auditory/Language				
1. Appears overly sensitive to loud noises (e.g., bells, toilet flush).				
2. Is hard to understand when she or he speaks.				
3. Appears to have difficulty in understanding or paying attention to what is said to him or her.				
4. Easily distracted by sounds; seems to hear sounds that go unnoticed by others.				
5. Has trouble following 2-3 step commands.				
Emotional				
1. Does not accept changes in routine easily.				
2. Becomes easily frustrated.				
3. Difficulty getting along with other children.				
4. Apt to be impulsive, heedless, accident-prone.				
5. Easier to handle in small group or individually.				
6. Marked mood variations, tendency to outbursts or tantrums.				
7. Tends to withdraw from groups—plays on the outskirts.				
8. Has trouble making needs known in appropriate manner.				
9. Avoids eye contact.				

Academic Difficulties:

_____ Reading	_____ Distractible	_____ Slow writer	_____ Following directions
_____ Math	_____ Restless	_____ Poorly organized	_____ Remembering information
_____ Spelling	_____ Hyperactive	_____ Finishing tasks	_____ Short attention span

How concerned are you about the above checked problems?　　Not concerned　　Slightly　　Moderately　　Very

Questions/Comments:

Child's Name: _____ Birth Date: _____ Age: _____

Date Completed: _____ Parents' Name(s): _____ Phone: _____

Name of Case Manager/Therapist/Teacher: _____

Name of Early Intervention/Preschool: _____

Adult/Adolescent Checklist (Age Twelve and Up)

The following checklist provided by the Occupational Therapy Association - Watertown, P.C. will provide you with a very detailed evaluation of sensory integration issues. If the client demonstrates behaviors associated with sensory integration dysfunction (DSI), it may be necessary to seek further information through evaluation by a qualified occupational or physical therapist.

Child's Name: _____ Date: _____

Check areas of difficulty: underline specific problems and star (*) prominent difficulties. If child has overall difficulty in one category or shows several items in three or more categories, this may indicate a need for an occupational therapist evaluation.

Did you / do you?	Rating Scale					Examples/Comments
Sensitivity (Sensory Modulation)						
1. Blink at bright lights or seem irritated or fatigued by them?	5	4	3	2	1	
2. Become easily distracted by visual stimulation?	5	4	3	2	1	
3. Seem overly sensitive to sounds?	5	4	3	2	1	
4. Become distracted by lots of noise?	5	4	3	2	1	
5. Seek fast movement activities (e.g., hiking, skiing)?	5	4	3	2	1	
6. Avoid fast carnival rides that spin or go up and down?	5	4	3	2	1	
7. Become motion sick (e.g., in cars or airplanes)?	5	4	3	2	1	
8. Seem fearful of heights?	5	4	3	2	1	
9. React defensively or seem overly sensitive to odors (e.g., perfume, foods)?	5	4	3	2	1	
10. React defensively to the taste and texture of foods?	5	4	3	2	1	
11. Seem excessively ticklish?	5	4	3	2	1	
12. Prefer to touch rather than be touched?	5	4	3	2	1	
13. Feel bothered by clothes (eg., socks, turtlenecks, or pantyhose)?	5	4	3	2	1	
14. Avoid getting hands into messy things?	5	4	3	2	1	
15. Tend to be more sensitive to pain than others?	5	4	3	2	1	
16. Strongly dislike showers or become irritated when splashed?	5	4	3	2	1	
17. Dislike light touch from other people?	5	4	3	2	1	

Did you / do you?	Rating Scale					Examples/Comments
Spatial and Body Awareness (Sensory Discrimination)						
1. Have difficulty looking for items on a grocery shelf?	5	4	3	2	1	
2. Have difficulty interpreting drawings in comics or cartoons?	5	4	3	2	1	
3. Have difficulty following traffic signs while driving?	5	4	3	2	1	
4. Have difficulty listening when background noise is present in a movie theater or large gathering?	5	4	3	2	1	
5. Seem to have trouble remembering or understanding what is said?	5	4	3	2	1	
6. Unable to follow two or three verbal directions given at once?	5	4	3	2	1	
7. Have difficulty learning to ride a bike?	5	4	3	2	1	
8. Have difficulty merging while driving onto a freeway?	5	4	3	2	1	
9. Have difficulties with balance?	5	4	3	2	1	
10. Get lost in new or familiar places?	5	4	3	2	1	
11. Prefer foods with strong tastes?	5	4	3	2	1	
12. Have difficulty finding objects in your pocket or purse without looking?	5	4	3	2	1	
13. Have difficulty licking an ice cream cone?	5	4	3	2	1	
14. Bump into things frequently?	5	4	3	2	1	
15. Over- or underestimate amount of force needed for a task?	5	4	3	2	1	
16. Tend to break many objects?	5	4	3	2	1	

Did you / do you?	Rating Scale					Examples/Comments
Posture/Strength/Planning Ability						
1. Tire easily with physical activity or handwriting?	5	4	3	2	1	
2. Have difficulty sitting in class or at a meeting without excessively moving in your chair?	5	4	3	2	1	
3. Think of yourself as clumsy?	5	4	3	2	1	
4. Tend to be slow in eating?	5	4	3	2	1	
5. Have difficulty with motor tasks that have several steps?	5	4	3	2	1	
6. Take a long time to do most motor tasks; e.g., dressing?	5	4	3	2	1	
7. Have difficulty learning exercise steps or routines?	5	4	3	2	1	
Social/Emotional						
1. Tend to prefer to be alone?	5	4	3	2	1	
2. Have a strong desire for sameness and routine?	5	4	3	2	1	
3. Lack self-confidence?	5	4	3	2	1	
4. Have strong feelings of anger or rage?	5	4	3	2	1	
5. Tend to become easily frustrated?	5	4	3	2	1	
6. Have panic or anxiety attacks?	5	4	3	2	1	

©1999 Occupational Therapy Associates Watertown, P.C.

Do you have difficulty with any of the following? (Check those that apply)

_____ Reading   _____ Following directions   _____ Finishing tasks

_____ Math   _____ Remembering information   _____ Paying attention

_____ Spelling   _____ Sleep   _____ Sports

_____ Handwriting   _____ Recovering from stress   _____ Physical Education/Exercise class

_____ Organizing work _____ Restlessness

Questions/Comments:

How concerned are you about the above checked problems?   Not concerned   Slightly   Moderately   Very

Name: _____ Birth Date: _____ Age: _____

Date Completed: _____ Parents' Name(s): _____ Phone: _____

Name of Case Manager/Therapist/Teacher: _____

Name of Referring agency/school: _____

Balzer-Martin Preschool Screening—Teachers Checklist

When concerned about an individual child, make several copies of this checklist and distribute it to school professionals acquainted with the child. Use the completed forms as the basis for a conversation about how to best serve the needs of a child.

As with the other checklists in this booklet, this screening tool quickly helps the reader gain an understanding of common signs and symptoms. Sensory integrative challenges can further be assessed through standardized methods, but screening tools such as this one are a good place to begin. Consult your school occupational or physical therapist for more information on standardized assessment, or call the American Occupational Therapy Association (see "organizations" in the resources section of this booklet for contact information).

Child's Name: _____ Age (yrs & mos): _____

Teachers: _____ / _____ Date: _____

Compared to his/her peers, is this child ADEQUATE in:

1. Ability to tolerate light and/or unexpected touch?   ☐ Yes ☐ No

    Comments:

2. Willing participation in messy activities (e.g., sand, fingerpaints, etc.)?   ☐ Yes ☐ No

    Comments:

3. Ability to sit upright in a chair without slouching or sprawling over the table?   ☐ Yes ☐ No

    Comments:

4. Ability to enjoy or participate in intense movement experiences such as swinging high, bouncing vigorously, or spinning around?   ☐ Yes ☐ No

    Does s/he avoid such experiences?   ☐ Yes ☐ No

    Does s/he crave such experiences, possibly not getting dizzy?   ☐ Yes ☐ No

    Comments:

5. Ability to get outer clothing on and off?   ☐ Yes ☐ No

    Comments:

6. Ability to move body in smooth, coordinated manner (i.e., not moving in an awkward or unusual way)?   ☐ Yes ☐ No

    Comments:

7. Use of both hands together when necessary (e.g., catching a ball, beating rhythm sticks, or holding a cup while pouring juice)?   ☐ Yes ☐ No

    Comments:

8. Consistent preference for using one hand when working with markers, crayons, or pencils? (age four and up) _ Left _ Right   ☐ Yes ☐ No

    Comments:

9. Ability to work with a marker, crayon or pencil? ☐ Yes ☐ No

   Comments:

10. Ability to work with scissors? ☐ Yes ☐ No

    Comments:

11. Ability to maintain sufficient attention span for things s/he enjoys? ☐ Yes ☐ No

    Comments:

12. Ability to remain calm during routine classroom activities without becoming restless or fidgety?
    ☐ Yes ☐ No

    Comments:

13. Ability to eat and chew normally, without noticeable difficulties such as being excessively messy, refusing certain textures, or cramming food in mouth? ☐ Yes ☐ No

    Comments:

In comparing this child with his/her peers, do you see PROBLEMS such as:

14. Overflow of movement in body parts not directly involved in an activity (e.g., tongue protrusion, jaw motion, movements in non-dominant hand, etc.)? ☐ Yes ☐ No

    Comments:

15. Over-sensitivity to noises (e.g., putting hands over ears or complaining about sounds when others are not bothered)? ☐ Yes ☐ No

    Comments:

16. Vision stress (e.g., inattentiveness when drawing or doing puzzles; insistence on "sameness" in day-to-day activities; lack of good, consistent eye contact; excessive shyness; unusual awkwardness)? ☐ Yes ☐ No

    Comments:

17. Auditory language difficulties (e.g., when following directions, looks to others for cues before responding; has difficulty changing or rephrasing verbalizations when s/he is not understood; gives short or very limited verbal responses; cannot recall names of people or objects)?
    ☐ Yes ☐ No

    Comments:

18. Other behaviors that you feel may be atypical for his/her stage of development (e.g., drooling, stuttering, unusual postures or movements)? ☐ Yes ☐ No

    Comments:

Characteristics of Tactile Dysfunction

The following checklists will help you gauge whether your child has tactile dysfunction. As you check recognizable characteristics, you will begin to see emerging patterns that help to explain your child's out-of-sync behavior. Not all characteristics will apply, but many checked boxes suggest that SPD affects your child.

The sensory avoider with overresponsivity (tactile defensiveness) has difficulties with passive touch (being touched). He may:

☐ Respond negatively and emotionally to light touch sensations, exhibiting anxiety, hostility, or aggression. He may withdraw from light touch, scratching or rubbing the place that has been touched. As an infant, he may have rejected cuddling as a source of pleasure or calming.

☐ Respond negatively and emotionally to the possibility of light touch. He may appear irritable or fearful when others are close, as when lining up.

☐ Respond negatively and emotionally when approached from the rear, or when touch is out of his field of vision, such as when someone's foot grazes his under a blanket or table.

☐ Show fight-or-flight response when touched on the face, such as having his face washed.

☐ Respond negatively when hairs on his body (arms, legs, neck, face, back, etc.) are displaced and "rubbed the wrong way." A high wind or even a breeze can raise his hairs, literally "ruffling his feathers."

☐ Show fight-or-flight response to hair displacement, such as having his hair brushed, or receiving a haircut, shampoo, or pat on the head.

☐ Become upset in weather with rain, wind, or gnats.

☐ Be excessively ticklish.

☐ Overrespond to physically painful experiences, making a "big deal" over a minor scrape or a splinter. The child may remember and talk about such experiences for days. He may be a hypochondriac.

☐ Respond similarly to dissimilar touch sensations. A raindrop on his skin may cause as adverse a response as a thorn.

☐ Strongly resist being touched by a barber, dentist, nurse, or pediatrician.

☐ Exhibit behavior that seems stubborn, rigid, inflexible, willful, verbally or physically pushy, or otherwise "difficult" for no apparent reason, when it is actually an aversive response to tactile stimuli.

☐ Rebuff friendly or affectionate pats and caresses, especially if the person touching is not a parent or familiar person. The child may reject touch altogether from anyone except his mother (or primary caregiver).

☐ Be distracted, inattentive and fidgety when quiet concentration is expected.

☐ Prefer receiving a hug to a kiss. He may crave the deep touch pressure of a hug, but try to rub off the irritating light touch of a kiss.

☐ Resist having his fingernails trimmed.

☐ Dislike surprises.

The same sensory avoider with overresponsivity also has difficulties with active touch. He may:

☐ Resist brushing his teeth.

- ☐ Be a picky eater, preferring certain textures such as crispy or mushy foods. The child may dislike foods with unpredictable lumps, such as tomato sauce or vegetable soup, as well as sticky foods like rice and cake icing.

- ☐ Refuse to eat hot or cold food.

- ☐ Avoid giving kisses.

- ☐ Resist baths, or insist that bath water be extremely hot or cold.

- ☐ Curl or protect hands to avoid touch sensations.

- ☐ Be unusually fastidious, hurrying to wash a tiny bit of dirt off his hands.

- ☐ Avoid walking barefoot on grass or sand, or wading in water.

- ☐ Walk on tiptoe to minimize contact with the ground.

- ☐ Fuss about clothing, such as stiff new clothes, rough textures, shirt collars, turtlenecks, belts, elasticized waists, hats, and scarves.

- ☐ Fuss about footwear, particularly sock seams. He may refuse to wear socks. He may complain about shoelaces. He may insist upon wearing beach sandals on cold, wet, winter days, or heavy boots on hot summer days.

- ☐ Prefer short sleeves and shorts and refuse to wear hats and mittens, even in winter, to avoid the sensation of clothes rubbing on his skin.

- ☐ Prefer long sleeves and pants and insist on wearing hats and mittens, even in summer, to avoid having his skin exposed.

- ☐ Avoid touching certain textures or surfaces, like some fabrics, blankets, rugs, or stuffed animals.

- ☐ Need to touch repeatedly certain surfaces and textures that provide soothing and comforting tactile experiences, such as a favorite blanket.

- ☐ Withdraw from art, science, music and physical activities to avoid touch sensations.

- ☐ Avoid messy play, such as sand, fingerpaint, paste, glue, mud, and clay, perhaps becoming tearful at the idea.

- ☐ Stand still or move against the traffic in group activities such as obstacle courses or movement games, keeping constant visual tabs on others.

- ☐ Treat pets roughly, or avoid physical contact with pets.

- ☐ Arm himself at all times with a stick, toy, rope, or other hand-held weapon.

- ☐ Rationalize verbally, in socially acceptable terms, why he avoids touch sensations, i.e., "My mother told me not to get my hands dirty," or "I'm allergic to mashed potatoes."

- ☐ Withdraw from a group and resist playing at other children's homes.

- ☐ Have trouble forming warm attachments with others. Experiencing difficulty in social situations, he may be a loner, with few close friends.

The sensory disregarder with underresponsivity may show atypical responses to passive and active touch. The child may:

- ☐ Not notice touch unless it is very intense.

- ☐ Be unaware of messiness on his face, especially around his mouth and nose, not noticing a crumby face or a runny nose.

- ☐ Be unaware of mussed hair or mulch or sand in hair.

- ☐ Not notice that clothes are in disarray, or that cuffs and socks are wet.

- ☐ Not notice heat, cold, or changes in temperature indoors or out, often keeping on a jacket even when sweating, or not reaching for a jacket even when shivering.

- ☐ Show little or no response to pain from scrapes, bruises, cuts, or shots, perhaps shrugging off a broken finger or collarbone.

- ☐ When barefoot, not complain about sharp gravel, hot sand, or stubbed toes.

- ☐ Not react to spicy, peppery, acidic, hot or "mouth-burning" food—or, on the other hand, may crave this kind of food.

- ☐ Be oblivious to weather conditions with wind, rain, or gnats.

- ☐ Fail to realize that he has dropped something.

- ☐ Not move away when leaned on or crowded.

- ☐ Appear to lack "inner drive" to touch, handle and explore toys and materials that appeal to most other children.

- ☐ Require intense tactile stimulation to become engaged in the world around him, but not actively seek it.

- ☐ Hurt other children or pets during play, seemingly without remorse, but actually not comprehending the pain that others feel.

The sensory craver with sensory seeking needs extra touch stimuli, both passive and active. The child may:

- ☐ Ask for tickles or back rubs.

- ☐ Enjoy vibration or movement that provides strong sensory feedback.

- ☐ Need to touch and feel everything in sight, e.g., bumping and touching others and running hands over furniture and walls. The child "gotta touch" items that other children understand are not to be touched.

- ☐ Rub certain textures over his arms and legs to get light touch input.

- ☐ Rub or even bite his own skin excessively.

- ☐ Constantly twirl hair in fingers.

- ☐ Frequently remove socks and shoes.

- ☐ Seem compelled to touch or walk barefoot on certain surfaces and textures that other people find uncomfortable or painful.

- ☐ Seek certain messy experiences, often for long durations.

- ☐ Seek very hot or cool room temperature and bath water.

- ☐ Have high tolerance for sweltering summer or freezing winter weather.

- ☐ "Dive" into food, often cramming mouth with food.

- ☐ Prefer steaming hot, icy cold, extra-spicy, or excessively sweet foods.

- ☐ Use his mouth to investigate objects, even after the age of two. (The mouth provides more intense information than hands.)

- ☐ Show "in your face" behavior, getting very close to others and touching them, even if his touches are unwelcome.

The child having a problem with tactile discrimination may:

☐ Have poor body awareness and not know where his body parts are or how they relate to one another. He may seem "out of touch" with hands, feet, and other body parts, as if they are unfamiliar attachments.

☐ Be unable to identify which body parts have been touched without looking.

☐ Have trouble orienting his arms and hands, legs and feet to get dressed.

☐ Be unable to identify familiar objects solely through touch, needing the additional help of vision, e.g., when reaching for objects in a pocket, box, or desk.

☐ Be unable to know the difference between similar items he is using, such as a crayon versus a marker.

☐ Be disheveled, with shoes on wrong feet, socks sagging, shoelaces untied, waistband twisted, and shirt untucked.

☐ Avoid initiating tactile experiences, such as picking up toys, materials and tools that are attractive to others.

☐ Have trouble perceiving the physical properties of objects, such as their texture, shape, size, temperature, or density.

☐ Be fearful in the dark.

☐ Prefer standing to sitting, in order to ensure visual control of his surroundings.

☐ Act silly in the classroom, playing the role of "class clown."

☐ Have a limited imagination.

☐ Have a limited vocabulary because of inexperience with touch sensations.

The child with dyspraxia may:

☐ Have trouble conceiving of, organizing, and performing activities that involve a sequence of movements, such as cutting, pasting, coloring, assembling collage pieces or recipe ingredients, applying nail polish, and so forth. Novel experiences as well as familiar activities may be difficult.

☐ Have poor gross-motor control for running, climbing, and jumping.

☐ Have poor eye-hand coordination.

☐ Require visual cues to perform certain motor tasks that other children can do without looking, such as zipping, snapping, buttoning and unbuttoning clothes.

☐ Put on gloves or socks in unusual ways.

☐ Have poor fine-motor control of his fingers for precise manual tasks, e.g., holding and using eating utensils and classroom tools, such as crayons, scissors, staplers, and hole punchers.

☐ Struggle with handwriting, drawing, completing worksheets and similar tasks.

☐ Have poor fine-motor control of his toes for walking barefoot or in flip-flops.

☐ Have poor fine-motor control of his mouth muscles for sucking, swallowing, chewing, and speaking.

☐ Be a messy eater.

☐ Have poor self-help skills and not be a "self-starter," requiring another person's help to get going.

Characteristics of Vestibular Dysfunction

These checklists will help you gauge whether your child has vestibular dysfunction. As you check recognizable characteristics, you will begin to see emerging patterns that help to explain your child's out-of-sync behavior.

The overresponsive child who shows intolerance for movement may:

☐ Dislike playground activities, such as swinging, spinning, and sliding.

☐ Be cautious, slow-moving, and sedentary, hesitating to take risks.

☐ Appear to be a sissy.

☐ Seem willful and uncooperative.

☐ Be very uncomfortable in elevators and on escalators, perhaps experiencing motion sickness.

☐ Demand continual physical support from a trusted adult.

The child with gravitational insecurity may:

☐ Have a great fear of falling, even where no real danger exists. This fear is experienced as primal terror.

☐ Be fearful of heights, even slightly raised surfaces. The child may avoid walking on a curb or jumping down from the bottom step.

☐ Become anxious when her feet leave the ground, feeling that even the smallest movement will throw her into outer space.

☐ Be fearful of climbing or descending stairs, and hold tightly to the banister.

☐ Feel threatened when her head is inverted, upside-down or tilted, as when having her head shampooed over the sink.

☐ Be fearful when someone moves her, as when a teacher slides her chair closer to the table.

☐ For self-protection, try to manipulate her environment and other people.

☐ Have poor proprioception and poor visual discrimination.

The sensory disregarder with underresponsiveness to vestibular sensations may:

☐ Not notice or object to being moved.

☐ Seem to lack inner drive to move actively.

☐ Once started, swing for a lengthy time without getting dizzy.

☐ Not notice sensation of falling and may not respond efficiently to protect himself by extending his hands or a foot to catch himself.

The sensory-seeking child with increased tolerance for movement may:

☐ Need to keep moving, as much as possible, in order to function. The child may have trouble sitting still or staying in a seat.

☐ Repeatedly, vigorously shake her head, rock back and forth, and jump up and down.

☐ Crave intense movement experiences, such as bouncing on furniture, using a rocking chair, turning in a swivel chair, assuming upside-down positions, or placing her head on the floor and pivoting around it.

☐ Be a "thrill seeker," enjoying fast-moving or spinning playground equipment, or seeking the fast and "scary" rides at an amusement park.

☐ Not get dizzy, even after twirling or spinning rapidly for a lengthy amount of time.

☐ Enjoy swinging very high and/or for long periods of time.

☐ Like seesaws, teeter-totters, or trampolines more than other children.

The sensory slumper with sensory-based postural disorder affecting movement of the head, balance, muscle tone, and bilateral coordination may:

☐ Lose her balance unless both feet are firmly planted, as when stretching on tiptoes, jumping, or standing on both feet when her eyes are closed.

☐ Easily lose her balance when out of a biped (two-footed) position, as when climbing stairs, riding a bicycle, hopping, on standing on one foot.

☐ Move in an uncoordinated, awkward way.

☐ Be fidgety and clumsy.

☐ Have a loose and floppy body.

☐ Feel limp (like a wet noodle) when you lift her, move her limbs to help her get dressed, or try to help her balance on a teeter-totter or balance beam.

☐ Tend to slump or sprawl in a chair or over a table, prefer to lie down rather than sit upright, and constantly lean her head on a hand or arm.

☐ Find it hard to hold up her head, arms, and legs simultaneously when lying on her stomach.

☐ Sit on the floor with her legs in a "W," i.e., with her knees bent and her feet extended out to the sides, to stabilize her body.

☐ Have difficulty turning door knobs or handles that require pressure, and have a loose grasp on "tools" such as pencils, scissors, or spoons.

☐ Have a tight, tense grasp on objects (to compensate for looseness).

☐ Have problems with digestion and elimination, such as frequent constipation or poor bladder control.

☐ Fatigue easily during physical activities or family outings.

☐ Be unable to catch herself from falling.

☐ Not have crawled or crept as a baby.

☐ Have poor body awareness.

☐ Have poor gross-motor skills and frequently stumble and trip, or be clumsy at sports and active games. She may seem to have "two left feet."

☐ Have poor fine-motor skills and difficulty using "tools" such as eating utensils, crayons, pencils, and combs.

☐ Have difficulty making both feet or both hands work together, such as when jumping up and down or throwing and catching a ball.

☐ Have difficulty using one foot or hand to assist the other during tasks such as standing on one foot to kick a ball, or holding the paper steady when writing or cutting.

☐ Have trouble using both hands in a smooth, alternating manner, as when striking rhythm instruments together to keep a musical beat.

☐ Not have an established hand preference by the age of 4 or 5. The child may use either hand for coloring and writing, or may switch the crayon or pencil from one hand to the other.

- ☐ Avoid crossing the midline. The child may switch the brush from hand to hand while painting a horizontal line, or may have trouble tapping a hand on her opposite shoulder in games like "Simon Says."

- ☐ Have a hard time with organization and structured activities.

The sensory fumbler with dyspraxia (poor motor planning) may:

- ☐ Have difficulty conceptualizing, organizing, and carrying out a sequence of unfamiliar movements.

- ☐ Be unable to generalize what she has already learned in order to accomplish a new task.

The child who is emotionally insecure may:

- ☐ Get easily frustrated and give up quickly.

- ☐ Be reluctant to try new activities.

- ☐ Have a low tolerance for potentially stressful situations.

- ☐ Have low self-esteem.

- ☐ Be irritable in others' company, and avoid or withdraw from people.

- ☐ Have difficulty making friends and relating to peers.

Characteristics of Proprioceptive Dysfunction

These checklists will help you gauge whether your child has proprioceptive dysfunction. As you check recognizable characteristics, you will begin to see emerging patterns that explain your child's out-of-sync behavior.

The child who is overresponsive to proprioceptive input may:

☐ Prefer not to move.

☐ Become upset when limbs are passively moved.

☐ Become upset when it is necessary to stretch or contract his muscles.

☐ Avoid weight-bearing activities, such as jumping, hopping, running, crawling, rolling, and other physical actions that bring strong proprioceptive input to muscles.

☐ Be a picky eater.

The underresponsive child may:

☐ Have low tone.

☐ "Fix" elbow to ribs when writing, or knees tightly together when standing, to compensate for low muscle tone.

☐ Break toys easily.

The sensory seeking child may:

☐ Deliberately "bump and crash" into objects in the environment, e.g., jump from high places, dive into a leaf pile, and tackle people.

☐ Stamp or slap his feet on ground when walking.

☐ Kick his heels against the floor or chair.

☐ Bang a stick or other object on a wall or fence while walking.

☐ To modulate his arousal level, engage in self-stimulatory activities, such as head banging, nail biting, finger sucking, or knuckle cracking.

☐ Rub his hands repeatedly on tables.

☐ Like to be tightly swaddled in a blanket or tucked in tightly at bedtime.

☐ Prefer shoelaces, hoods, and belts to be tightly fastened.

☐ Chew constantly on objects, such as shirt collars and cuffs, hood strings, pencils, toys, and gum. The child may enjoy chewy foods.

☐ Appear to be aggressive.

The child with poor discrimination, postural disorder and dyspraxia may:

☐ Have poor body awareness and motor control.

☐ Have difficulty planning and executing movement. Controlling and monitoring motor tasks such as adjusting a collar or putting on eyeglasses may be especially hard if the child cannot see what he is doing.

☐ Have difficulty positioning his body, as when someone is helping him into a coat, or when he is trying to dress or undress himself.

☐ Have difficulty knowing where his body is in relation to objects and people, frequently falling, tripping, and bumping into obstacles.

☐ Have difficulty going up and down stairs.

☐ Show fear when moving in space.

The child with inefficient grading of movement may:

☐ Flex and extend his muscles more or less than necessary for tasks such as inserting his arms into sleeves, or climbing.

☐ Hold pencils and crayons too lightly to make a clear impression, or so tightly that the points break.

☐ Produce messy written work, often with large erasure holes.

☐ Frequently break delicate objects, and seem like a "bull in a china shop."

☐ Break items that require simple manipulation, such as lamp switches, hair barrettes, and toys that require putting together and pulling apart.

☐ Pick up an object, such as a glass of milk, with more force than necessary, causing the object to fly through the air.

☐ Pick up an object with less force than necessary—and thus be unable to lift it. He may complain that objects such as boots or toys are "too heavy."

☐ Have difficulty lifting or holding objects if they don't weigh the same. He may not understand concepts of "heavy" and "light."

The child with sensory-based postural disorder may:

☐ Have poor posture.

☐ Lean his head on his hands when he works at a desk.

☐ Slump in a chair, over a table, or while seated on the floor.

☐ Sit on the edge of the chair and keep one foot on the floor for extra stability.

☐ Be unable to keep his balance while standing on one foot.

The child with emotional insecurity may:

☐ Avoid participation in ordinary movement experiences, because they make him feel uncomfortable or inadequate.

☐ Become rigid, sticking to the activities that he has mastered and resisting new challenges.

☐ Lack self-confidence, saying, "I can't do that," even before trying.

☐ Become timid in unfamiliar situations.

Characteristics of Visual Dysfunction

These checklists will help you gauge whether your child has visual dysfunction. As you check recognizable characteristics, you will begin to see emerging patterns that help to explain your child's out-of-sync behavior.

The child with a problem with basic visual skills may:

☐ Have headaches, eye strain, or red, burning, itchy, or teary eyes.

☐ Rub eyes or blink, frown, and squint excessively.

☐ Complain about blurred images when looking at pictures, print, or faces.

☐ Complain of seeing double.

☐ Complain that words seem to move on the page.

☐ Turn or tilt her head as she reads across a page.

☐ Hold a book too closely, or lower her face too closely to the desk.

☐ Have difficulty seeing the storybook or chalkboard, and request to move nearer.

☐ Have difficulty shifting her gaze from one object to another, such as when looking from the blackboard to her own paper, and make errors in copying.

☐ Have difficulty focusing on stationary objects.

☐ Frequently lose her place on the page, reread words or lines, and omit numbers, letters, words, or lines when reading or writing, and need to use her finger to keep her place.

☐ Have difficulty tracking or following a moving object, such as a ping-pong ball, or following along a line of printed words.

☐ Fatigue easily during schoolwork and sports-related activities.

The child with difficulty modulating visual sensations may:

☐ Shield her eyes to screen out sights, close or cover one eye, or squint.

☐ Avoid bright lights and sunlight, perhaps preferring to wear sunglasses, even indoors.

☐ Be uncomfortable or overwhelmed by moving objects or people.

☐ Duck or try to avoid objects coming toward her, such as a ball or another child.

☐ Withdraw from classroom participation and avoid group movement activities.

☐ Avoid direct eye contact.

☐ Experience headaches, nausea, or dizziness when using eyes.

☐ Be unaware of light/dark contrast, edges, and reflections.

☐ Be unaware of movement, often bumping into moving objects such as swings.

☐ Respond late to visual information, such as obstacles in her path.

☐ Seek bright lights, strobe lights and direct sunlight.

☐ Seek visual stimulation, such as finger flicking, spinning, peering at patterns and edges such as ceiling and fence lines.

☐ Move excessively (squirm, fidget) during visual tasks, such as workbook activities.

The child with poor visual discrimination may:

- ☐ Have difficulty seeing objects in three dimensions (depth perception).

- ☐ Seem overwhelmed by moving objects or people because of a problem discriminating between what moves and what is motionless (stable visual field).

- ☐ Have difficulty judging relative distances between objects, such as letters, words, numbers or drawings on a page; between oneself and objects in the environment, often bumping into things (spatial relationships).

- ☐ Not understand concepts such as up/down, forward/back, before/after, and first/second (spatial relationships). The child may have a problem stringing beads in order, following a pattern to build with blocks, or wayfinding (going from one place to another without getting lost, or finding one's way in a new place).

- ☐ Have difficulty in team sports that require awareness of position on the field or court and knowledge of teammates' positions and movements.

- ☐ Confuse likenesses and differences in pictures, words, symbols, and objects and have difficulty distinguishing properties of objects.

- ☐ Repeatedly confuse similar beginnings and endings of words ("tree/three," "fight/flight/fright," "window/winter").

- ☐ Have difficulty with schoolwork involving the size of letters, the spacing of letters and words on the line, and the lining up of numbers (form constancy). The child may reverse letters ("b/d") or words ("saw/was") while reading and writing.

- ☐ Have difficulty differentiating objects in the foreground and background, necessary to distinguish one word on a page, or a face in a crowd (visual figure-ground).

- ☐ Be unable to form mental images of objects, people, or scenarios, to envision what she reads or hears, or relate pictures and words to the "real thing" (visualization).

- ☐ Have difficulty describing thoughts and actions, both verbally and in writing.

- ☐ Be a poor speller.

- ☐ Have difficulty remembering what he did or saw during the day.

- ☐ Be unable to interpret how objects would feel, just by looking at them; the child must touch the kitten to know it is soft and furry.

- ☐ Fail to comprehend what she is reading, or quickly lose interest.

- ☐ Have a short attention span for reading or copying information from the board, and have a poor visual memory of what she read.

The child with poor visual-motor skills may:

- ☐ Have poor eye-hand coordination—the efficient teamwork of the eyes and hands, necessary for playing with toys, using tools, dressing, writing, and academic tasks.

- ☐ Be unable to use her eyes to guide hand movements necessary for accurate orientation of drawings and words on a page. She may be unable to stay within the lines when she colors, and her writing may be crooked and poorly spaced.

- ☐ Have difficulty with fine-motor tasks involving spatial relationships, such as doing jigsaw puzzles, rearranging dollhouse furniture, and cutting along lines.

- ☐ Have poor eye-foot coordination and difficulty walking upstairs or kicking a ball.

- ☐ Have poor gross-motor skills and difficulty moving on playground equipment, such as reaching for and climbing on monkey bars.

- ☐ Avoid sports and group activities in which movement is required.
- ☐ Have difficulty with rhythmic activities.
- ☐ Have poor coordination and balance.
- ☐ Have difficulty sounding out a word silently and then saying it, or she may mispronounce similar words as she continues reading (eye-ear coordination).
- ☐ Orient drawings poorly on the page, or write uphill or downhill.
- ☐ Have exceedingly poor posture while at the table or desk, or twist in an unusual way to see the teacher or book.
- ☐ Withdraw from classroom participation.
- ☐ Have low self-esteem.

Characteristics of Auditory Dysfunction

These checklists will help you gauge whether your child has auditory dysfunction. As you check recognizable characteristics, you will begin to see emerging patterns that help to explain your child's out-of-sync behavior.

The child with difficulty modulating auditory sensations may:

☐ Be distressed by loud noises, including the sound of voices.

☐ Be distressed by sudden noises, such as thunder, fire alarms, sirens, or popping balloons.

☐ Be distressed by tinny or metallic sounds, such as those coming from a xylophone or from clinking silverware.

☐ Be distressed by high-pitched sounds, such as those coming from whistles, violins, sopranos, and screeching chalk.

☐ Be distressed by sounds that do not bother others, such as a toilet flushing, a distant church bell, or soft background music.

With poor auditory discrimination, the child may:

☐ Seem unaware of the source of sounds or may look all around to locate where they come from.

☐ Have difficulty recognizing particular sounds, such as voices or cars coming down the street.

☐ Have difficulty tracking a sound in the environment, such as footsteps.

☐ Have difficulty recalling, repeating, and referring to words, phrases, conversations, song lyrics, or instructions, both right away (immediate memory) and later (deferred memory).

☐ Have difficulty recognizing the difference between sounds, such as near or distant banging, angry or pleasant voices, or high or low notes.

☐ Be unable to focus or maintain attention to a voice, conversation, story, or sound without being distracted by other sounds.

☐ Have difficulty associating new sounds to familiar sounds, or visual symbols (letters, numerals, musical notes) to their particular sounds.

☐ Have difficulty hearing or reading jokes, verbal math problems, crossword puzzle definitions, or discussions and understanding how all the information fits together.

☐ Have a poor sense of timing and rhythm when clapping, marching, singing, jumping rope, or playing rhythm band instruments.

The child may also have difficulty with receptive language, and may:

☐ Have a problem discriminating similar-sounding word sounds, especially consonants at ends of words, as in cap/cat, bad/bag, side/sign.

☐ Have a short attention span for listening to stories or for reading.

☐ Misinterpret questions and requests.

☐ Be able to follow only one or two instructions in sequence.

☐ Look to others before responding.

☐ Frequently ask for repetition, or be less likely than others to ask for clarification of ambiguous directions or descriptions.

☐ Have difficulty recognizing rhymes.

☐ Have difficulty learning new languages.

The child may have difficulty with expressive language, and may:

☐ Have been a late talker.

☐ Have difficulty putting thoughts into spoken or written words.

☐ Talk "off topic," e.g., talk about her new shirt when others are discussing zoo animals or a soccer game.

☐ Have difficulty "closing circles of communication," i.e., responding to others' questions and comments on demand.

☐ Have difficulty correcting or revising what she has said so that others can understand.

☐ Have a weak vocabulary.

☐ Use immature sentence structure (poor grammar and syntax).

☐ Have poor spelling skills.

☐ Have a limited imagination in fantasy play.

☐ Have difficulty making up rhymes.

☐ Sing out of tune.

☐ Have difficulty with reading, especially out loud.

☐ Require more time than other children to respond to sounds and voices.

The child may have difficulty with speech and articulation, and may:

☐ Be unable to speak clearly enough to be understood.

☐ Have a flat, monotonous voice quality.

☐ Speak very loudly or very softly.

☐ Speak with a hoarse, husky, strident, weak or breathy voice.

☐ Speak hesitantly or without fluency and rhythm.

In general, the child may:

☐ Be tired at the end of the day.

☐ Have little motivation or interest in school work.

☐ Have difficulty planning tasks and getting organized.

☐ Be awkward and uncoordinated in movement.

☐ Have poor timing and poor athletic skills.

☐ Have low self-esteem.

☐ Be shy and tend to withdraw from social scenes.

☐ Improve the ability to speak while or after experiencing intense movement.

Heavy Work Activities List for Teachers

Compiled and Edited by Elizabeth Haber, MS, OTR/L and Deanna Iris Sava, MS, OTR/L

Following are activities school teams can use to provide heavy work activities for students. All the activities on this handout are "naturally occurring activities." This means they can be easily incorporated into the student's daily routine within the school environment. Special thanks to all the therapists who openly shared ideas!

1. Place chairs on desks at end of day or take down at beginning of day.

2. Erase the chalkboard/dry erase board.

3. Wash desks and/or chalkboard/dry erase board.

4. Help rearrange desks in the classroom.

5. Help the janitor with emptying wastebaskets, mopping the floor, etc.

6. Fill egg crates (small ones that students can carry) with books to take to other classrooms. Teachers could ask students to move these crates back and forth as needed.

7. Help the gym teacher move mats, hang them up, etc.

8. Take chewy candy breaks—such as licorice, fruit roll-ups, Starburst® or Tootsie Rolls.®

9. Take crunchy food breaks—such as dry cereal, vegetables, pretzels or popcorn.

10. Sharpen pencils with a manual sharpener.

11. Cut out items for display from oak tag.

12. Have students carry heavy notebooks to the office or from class to class.

13. Carry books with both hands hugging the book to the chest.

14. Push the lunch cart or carry lunch bin to the cafeteria.

15. Staple paper onto bulletin boards.

16. In the classroom, fasten a large phone book to the bottom of the student's chair with heavy duty tape. The teacher can rearrange the student' s schedule so the student has to move to a different location within the classroom (carrying or pushing his/her weighted chair) between certain subjects or activities.

17. Have student move several packs at a time of Xerox paper from the storage area to the school copy center.

18. Use the Ellison cut-out machine. Students can collect orders from teachers (who provide the paper and use these cut-outs for bulletin boards, etc.) and then press out the number of pieces required under the supervision of an adult. This very heavy work is a great strategy for organizing behavior.

19. Climb on playground equipment.

20. Swing from the trapeze bar.

21. Perform sports activities that involve running and jumping.

22. Run around the track at school.

23. Have students push against a wall. For younger students, you can use the idea that "The room feels small this morning—can everyone help me push the walls out to make the room bigger."

24. Fill up big toy trucks with heavy blocks, push with both hands to knock things down.

25. Have the student color a "rainbow" with large paper on the floor while on hands and knees.

26. Play "cars" under a table in the classroom where the student pushes the car with one hand while creeping and weight bearing on the other hand.

27. Open doors for people

28. Use squeeze toys that can be squeezed quietly on the student's lap under the desk so that the student does not disturb the class.

29. Do chair pushups.

30. Do animal walks (crab walk, bear walk, army crawl).

31. Jump on a mini-trampoline.

32. Stack chairs.

33. Take isometric exercise breaks.

Glossary

Attention Deficit Disorder (ADD) A neurological problem affecting attention. At times the child may be distracted by everything around her, while at other times she may have an unrelenting drive to engage in preferred activities for long periods of time. The child with ADD may be impulsive and easily frustrated. In addition, if the child just can't stop fidgeting and moving, the problem is called Attention Deficit with Hyperactivity (ADHD).

Auditory Defensiveness Hypersensitivity to noises and sounds not usually considered bothersome to other people. The sounds from vacuum cleaners, tea kettles, radio and television, certain kinds of music, sudden loud noises, or even certain people's voices can range from annoying to painful. Some children will cover their ears when they hear what they perceive to be irritating sounds.

Arousal Level (see **Modulation**) Term used synonymously with levels of modulation or stimulation.

Disinhibition Some people are unable, or inconsistently able, to screen out unimportant sensory information. Disinhibition of the screening mechanism of the brain (see Inhibition) can feel almost intolerable. One child described how he felt about being unable to filter this bombardment of sensory information. He said, "There's a traffic jam in my head."

Dyspraxia Trouble learning the steps in a new skill and difficulty performing this skill smoothly and automatically. Shoe tying, dressing, and mealtime skills may be difficult for the child to acquire, as well as to refine. Often, children with dyspraxia can do a skill easily one day and be unable to do it the next day. One child commented, after throwing a ball well, "How did I DO that?"

Fight, Flight, Freeze, or Fright Response Responding to ordinary, everyday happenings, not just raging bulls and speeding trucks, as if they were life threatening. The child may react by fighting, running away, panicking so she can't move, or crying in fear. The fight, flight, freeze, or fright response is the behavioral by-product of our autonomic nervous system's response to a real or perceived threat.

Filtering An instinctive, preconscious skill that makes it possible to scan the environment and selectively screen out nonessential or distracting sensory information.

Gravitational Insecurity Fear of being off the ground, sometimes to the extent of panicking. If severe, the person may feel as if he is falling if his head is tipped back. Children with this problem often have poor integration of the senses in the inner ear, muscles, and joints, which are so vital for a good relationship to gravity. Please refer to "Proprioception" and "Vestibular System" in this glossary.

Hypersensitivity Acute awareness of the environment, sometimes to the point of pain. Although one sense may be more "raw" to the environment than another, there is frequently hypersensitivity in most of the basic senses: smell, touch, movement, vision, and hearing. A person who is very sensitive may react with avoidance or with strong aversion.

Hyposensitivity "Muffled" or dampened sensory awareness of the environment. This diminished sensory perception manifests as an unusually high tolerance for typically aversive stimuli, such as acute pain or loud noise. To truly assess hyposensitivity, pathological causes, such as nerve damage, must be ruled out.

IDEA The Individuals with Disabilities Education Act, PL 99-457, and amendments. This law states that school districts must provide appropriate services for students identified as requiring assistance to achieve educational performance needs.

Inhibition There is so much going on around us all the time that our nervous system couldn't possibly handle it all without "malfunctioning." Inhibition, a critical function of the nervous system, is the ability to screen out unimportant sensory information to prevent sensory overload (see Disinhibition) A sensory diet can be planned to provide activities for inhibition.

Learning Disorder Challenges with learning to read, write, or do math that can't be accounted for by straightforward problems with vision, hearing, or lack of exposure to educational programs. Alternative educational approaches are often needed, and should be tailored to play to the child's strengths as a means of engaging the child in successful learning experiences.

Modulation The ability of the nervous system to have a "middle ground" or "comfort zone" of regulation as the person interacts with the challenges of daily life. A child with a sensory processing problem may have poor modulation with a narrow "comfort zone."

Motor Planning / Praxis The fluent synchrony of thought and movement resulting in organized, intentional action. Purposeful movement is praxis in action. When someone has a well-developed sense of praxis, his intuitive understanding of how to move or manipulate objects reflects this fluent synchrony of thought and action. People who are dyspraxic, or lack a well developed sense of praxis, will often develop compensatory thinking strategies requiring much more thought, planning, and organization to accomplish novel movement tasks.

Proprioception This term combines the Latin word "proprio," which translates to "within the body," and the English word "receptive." It is the awareness of ourselves gained through muscles and joints and through other receptors within our own bodies.

Self-Regulation see **Modulation**

Sensory Diet The individual person's specific "inhibition" or "facilitation" activities strategically planned throughout the day to deal with stress, keeping the nervous system in a state of balance (see **Modulation**). Inhibition activities provide the nervous system with body-based ways of calming and organizing. Examples of activities for inhibition include pushups, bicycling, or running. Learning to self-assess and take the appropriate action to bring one's nervous system into a balanced state is an essential feature of the sensory diet concept.

Sensory Discrimination Taking in information through all our senses, then processing, filtering, and interpreting all these sensations with our bodies and minds as a base for development of a skill.

Sensory Integration see **Sensory Processing**

Sensory Modulation see **Modulation**

Sensory Processing The process of taking in information about the world around us with all our senses and from inside our own bodies. Through integrating and organizing the senses of vision, touch, movement, muscle sense, hearing, taste, and smell, we are able to interact comfortably and efficiently in work and play, and in caring for ourselves and others.

Tactile Referring to touch. Touch can be basic awareness of where and how a person has been touched, or it can involve more discriminative touch as a base for the development of a skill.

Tactile Defensiveness Responding to light or unexpected touch as if it were uncomfortable or threatening. It is a hypersensitive or aversive reaction to being touched that interferes with relating comfortably to other people. The child may object to having tags in the back of shirts, wearing "tickly" clothing, having hair washed or teeth brushed, or handling certain textures.

Undersensitivity see **Hyposensitivity**.

Vestibular System The sensory system with receptors in the inner ear. It responds to changes in head position to help us keep our balance. This system is constantly "checking in" with our eyes, muscles, and joints to keep us oriented to gravity and to how we balance and move our bodies.

Hyposensitivity "Muffled" or dampened sensory awareness of the environment. This diminished sensory perception manifests as an unusually high tolerance for typically aversive stimuli, such as acute pain or loud noise. To truly assess hyposensitivity, pathological causes, such as nerve damage, must be ruled out.

Resources

Catalogs

Sensory Resources
2500 Chandler Avenue, Suite 3
Las Vegas, NV 89120-4064
Telephone: (888) 357-5867 for free catalog
Fax: (702) 891-8899
Website: www.SensoryResources.com
Email: Info@SensoryResources.com

Award winning audiotapes, CDs, videos, and books related to sensory integration and sensory processing disorder. Therapeutic Songames® are useful in home, school, and clinical settings. Titles include *Building Bridges through Sensory Integration*, *The Sensory Connection*, *The Goodenoughs Get in Sync*, *Preschool Sensory Scan for Educators (Preschool SENSE)*, *The Out-of-Sync Child* video, *Getting Kids in Sync* video, *Songames for Sensory Integration*, *Making Sense of Sensory Integration*, *Answers to Questions Teachers Ask about Sensory Integration*, and many others. Sensory Resources also sponsors workshops for parents, teachers, and therapists on sensory processing disorder and related topics.

Abilitations
3155 Northwoods Parkway
Norcross, GA 30071
Telephone: (800) 850-8602
Fax: (800) 845-1535
Website: www.abilitations.com

Wonderful products for parents and professionals alike. Click on "Thera-talk Discussion Group" to join interactive message boards for conversations regarding special needs.

Belle Curve Records, Inc.

Belle Curve Records products are now available from Sensory Resources. See above.

FlagHouse, Inc.
601 FlagHouse Drive
Hasbrouck, NJ 07604-3116
Telephone: (800) 793-7900
Fax: (800) 793-7922
Website: www.flaghouse.com

This company carries products for children and adults with sensory processing problems. Flaghouse is especially well regarded for its environmental enhancement products that facilitate calming and focusing in clients with moderate to severe issues.

Future Horizons, Inc.
721 W. Abram Street
Arlington, TX 76013
Telephone (800) 489-0727
Fax (817) 277-2270
Website: www.FutureHorizons-Autism.com
mail: Info@futurehorizons-autism.com

Future Horizons is the world's largest publisher of resources on autism and Asperger's syndrome. Besides an extensive catalog of books and videotapes, Future Horizons sponsors conferences throughout the country each year.

Mealtimes Catalog
New Visions
1124 Roberts Mountain Road
Faber, VA 22938
Telephone: (800) 606-3665
Fax: (434) 361-1807
Website: www.new-vis.com

Mealtime activities and therapy materials. Wonderful resources for speech-language, oral-motor, and feeding concerns, as well as music and learning.

Optometric Extension Program Foundation, Inc. (OEP)
1921 East Carnegie Avenue, Suite 3-L
Santa Ana, CA 92705-5510
Telephone: (800) 424-8070
Fax: (949) 250-8157
Website: www.oep.org

Products and workshops related to improving visual motor skills.

Playaway Toy Company, Inc.
P.O. Box 247
Bear Creek, WI 54922
Telephone: (715) 752-4565, or toll free (888) 752-9929
Fax: (715) 752-4476
Website: www.playawaytoy.com
Email: therapis@frontiernet.net

Maker of the famous Rainy Day Indoor Playground. This innovative, educational, and developmentally sound equipment turns any standard doorway into an "energy-releasing, muscle-coordinating way to have fun." Interchangeable parts include swings, trapeze bar, glider, net, platform, and ladder. Requiring no tools to install, the set is portable and transportable from door to door or house to house. A therapist's dream come true, an educators most valuable tool, and a parent's life saver

PDP Products and Professional Development Programs
14524 61st Street Court North
Stillwater, MN 55082
Telephone: (651) 439-8865
Fax: (651) 439-0421
Website: www.pdppro.com

Developmental learning materials, sensory integration treatment products and publications, and continuing education seminars. Sells "Move 'n Sit" cushions.

Pocket Full of Therapy
P.O. Box 174
Morganville, NJ 07751
Telephone: (800) 736-8124
Fax: (732) 441-1422
Website: www.pfot.com

Unique collection of educational and therapeutic toys and materials for use in the clinic, at school, or at home.

Sensory Processing Disorder Network (SPD Network)
1901 W Littleton Boulevard
Littleton, CO 80120
Telephone: (303) 794-1182
Fax: (303) 798-2526
Website: www.spdnetwork.org

A great site full of resources to help everyone – parents, teachers, therapists, doctors – learn about sensory processing disorder. Find reliable, accurate information that has been reviewed by experts. The site also features links to parent support groups (SPD Parent Connections), conferences and workshops, and the SPD Resource Directory, which lists healthcare and educational professionals, community and other resources experienced in sensory issues. Find a professional in your area or register as a resource in this directory at no cost.

Sensory Comfort
P.O. Box 6589
Portsmouth, NH 03802-6589
Telephone: (888) 436-2622
Fax: (603) 436-8422
Website: www.sensorycomfort.com

An exciting company specializing in making life more comfortable for children and adults with sensory processing difficulties.

Southpaw Enterprises
P.O. Box 1047
Dayton, OH 45401
Telephone: (800) 228-1698
Fax: (937) 252-8502
Website: www.southpawenterprises.com

Therapy equipment and creative toys for use at home, in school, or in the clinic.

Therapro, Inc.
225 Arlington Street
Framingham, MA 01702-8732
Telephone: (800) 257-5376
Fax: (800) 268-6624
Website: www.theraproducts.com

Developmental learning materials, sensory integration treatment products, and publications.

Organizations

Administration on Developmental Disabilities
Administration for Children and Families
U.S. Department of Health and Human Services
Mail Stop HHH 405-D
370 L'Enfant Promenade SW
Washington, D.C. 20447
Telephone: (202) 690-6590
Fax: (202) 690-6904
Website: www.acf.hhs.gov/programs/add

Contact for information regarding federally funded programming specific to the prevention, diagnosis, and treatment of developmental disabilities.

The American Occupational Therapy Association, Inc. (AOTA)
P.O. Box 31220
Bethesda, MD 20824-1220
Telephone: (301) 652-2682
TDD: (800) 377-8555
Fax: (301) 652-7711
Website: www.aota.org

This professional organization promotes improved awareness of occupational therapy services.

American Speech-Language-Hearing Association (ASHA)
10801 Rockville Pike
Rockville, MD 20852
Telephone: (800) 638-8255
TTY: (301) 897-5700
Fax: (301) 571-0457
Website: www.asha.org

Information about speech therapy services, products, publications, and self-help groups.

Council for Exceptional Children (CEC)
1110 North Glebe Road, Suite 300
Arlington, VA 22201
Telephone: (888) 232-7733
TTY: (866) 915-5000
Fax: (703) 264-9494
Website: www.cec.sped.org

Support for those who educate or care for exceptional children, including children with disabilities and those who are gifted.

Developmental Delay Resources
5801 Beacon Street
Pittsburgh, PA 15217
Telephone: (800) 497-0944
Fax: (412) 422-1374
Website: www.devdelay.org

Non-profit organization dedicated to helping parents and professionals learn cutting-edge strategies in helping children with special needs. The DDR's membership directory is a comprehensive resource for networking parents and professionals interested in complementary treatment approaches. DDR also publishes a very useful quarterly newsletter.

KID Foundation (Foundation for Knowledge in Development)
1901 W Littleton Boulevard
Littleton, CO 80120
Telephone: (303) 794-1182
Fax: (303) 798-2526
Website: www.kidfoundation.org

Focuses on research, education, and advocacy related to sensory processing disorder. This organization sponsors ongoing scientific research, educational conferences, local support groups for parents, and the SPD Network (www.spdnetwork.org). The KID Foundation also works to get sensory processing disorder (SPD) listed in standard medical diagnostic manuals, which will help to ensure accurate diagnoses and appropriate treatment for those with SPD.

Learning Disabilities Association of America (LDA)
4156 Library Road
Pittsburgh, PA 15234-1349
Telephone: (412) 341-1515
Fax: (412) 344-0224
Website: www.ldanatl.org

Professional organization advocating for people with learning disabilities.

National Dissemination Center for Children and Youth with Disabilities (NICHCY)
P.O. Box 1492
Washington, DC 20013-1492
Telephone: (800) 695-0285
Fax: (202) 884-8441
Website: www.nichcy.org

Resource information on raising children with special needs.

Parent Network for the Post-Institutionalized Child (PNPIC)
P.O. Box 613
Meadowlands, PA 15347-0613
Website: www.pnpic.org
Email: PNPIC@aol.com

A parent-centered support and resource referral organization for parents who have adopted post-institutionalized children.

Porter Sargent Publishers, Inc.
300 Bedford Street, Suite 213
Manchester, NH 03102
Telephone: (800) 342-7470
Fax: (603) 669-7945
Website: www.portersargent.com

Publishers of *The Directory for Exceptional Children*. A comprehensive survey of 2,500 schools, facilities, and organizations across the United States serving children and young adults with developmental, emotional, physical, and medical disabilities. They also publish *The Guide to Summer Camps and Summer Schools* that includes information on programs for children with special needs.

Therapy Works, Inc.
4901 Butte Place NW
Albuquerque, NM 87120
Telephone: (877) 897-3478
Fax: (505) 899-4071
Website: www.alertprogram.com

Workshops to help parents and professionals learn about sensory integration and its impact on self-regulation. Therapy Works' cofounders, Mary Sue Williams MS, OTR/L and Sherry Shellenberger MS, OTR/L, developed a treatment model for children that is widely regarded as an effective method for teaching children how to assess and change their level of self-regulation through specific kinds of movement and sensory play activities.

Zero to Three
National Center for Infants, Toddlers, and Families
2000 M Street NW, Suite 200
Washington, DC 20036
Telephone: (800) 899-4301
Website: www.zerotothree.org

Educational organization geared toward training parents and professionals to encourage the physical, emotional, social, and cognitive growth of children from birth to three. Publishers of the *Zero to Three* journal.

References

Anderson, E., and P. Emmons. 1996. *Unlocking the mysteries of sensory dysfunction.* Arlington, TX: Future Horizons.

Ayres, A. J. 1972. *Sensory integration and learning disorders.* Los Angeles: Western Psychological Services.

———. 1975. *Sensorimotor foundations of academic ability.* In *Perceptual and learning disabilities in children. Vol. 2,* by W. M. Cruickshank and D. P. Hallahan. (Syracuse, NY: Syracuse University Press).

———. 1989. *The Sensory integration and praxis tests (SIPT).* Los Angeles: Western Psychological Services.

———. 2005. *Sensory integration and the child—Understanding hidden sensory challenges.* Revised and updated by Pediatric Therapy Network. Los Angeles. Western Psychological Services.

Balzer-Martin, L. A., and C. S. Kranowitz. *The Balzer-Martin preschool training manual.* (Available from St. Columba's Nursery School, 4201 Albemarle St. NW, Washington, DC 20016, Tel. 202-363-4121.)

Benbow, M. 1990. *Loops and other groups: A kinesthetic writing system.* San Antonio: Therapy Skill Builders.

Bowen-Irish, T. 1998. *OT treatment within an elementary inclusive classroom.* Baltimore: AOTA Annual Conference.

Brewer, C., and D. Campbell. 1991. *Rhythms of learning.* Phoenix: Zephyr Press.

Bundy, A. C., S. J. Lane, and E. A. Murray. 2002. *Sensory integration: Theory and practice.* 2d ed. Philadelphia: F.A. Davis.

Cermak, S., and V. Groza. 1998. *Sensory integration in post-institutionalized children: Implications for social workers. Child and Adolescent Social Work Journal* 16: 5-37.

Cermak, S. 1998. *The relationship between attention deficit and sensory integration disorders, Part 1. AOTA Sensory Integration Special Interest Newsletter* 11: 1-4.

Chandler, B., W. Dunn., and J. Rourk. 1989. *Guidelines for occupational therapy services in the school system.* 2d ed. Bethesda, MD: American Occupational Therapy Association.

Clark, F., Z. Mailloux, and D. Parham. 1989. *Sensory integration and children with learning disabilities.* In *Occupational therapy for children.* 2d ed, edited by P. N. Pratt and A. S. Allen (St. Louis: C.V. Mosby).

Cohn, E., and S. Cermak. 1998. *Research outcome measures in sensory integration. American Journal of Occupational Therapy* 52, no. 7: 540-546.

Coster, W., J. Dweeney., J. Haltiwander., and S. Haley. 1998. *School function assessment.* San Antonio, TX: Psychological Corporation.

Emberley, E. 1994. *Ed Emberley's drawing book of animals.* New York: Little, Brown and Co.

———. 1994. *Ed Emberley's great thumbprint drawing book.* New York: Little, Brown and Co.

Frick, S. M., and N. Lawton-Shirley. *Auditory integrative training from a sensory integrative perspective. AOTA Sensory Integration Special Interest Section Newsletter* 17. 4: 1-3.

Gardner, H. 1993. *Frames of mind: The theory of multiple intelligences.* New York: Basic Books.

Grandin, T. 1995. *Thinking in pictures.* New York: Doubleday.

Grandin, T., and M. Scariano. 1986. Emergence: labeled autistic. Novato, CA: Arena.

Greenspan, S. I., and N. T. Greenspan. 1985. *First feelings: Milestones in the emotional development of your child from birth to age four.* New York: Viking Penguin.

———. and N. T. Greenspan. 1989. *The essential partnership: How parents can meet the emotional challenges of infancy and childhood.* New York: Viking Penguin.

———. 1995. *The challenging child.* Reading, MA: Addison-Wesley.

———. and J. Salmon. 1993. *Playground politics: Understanding the emotional life of your school-age child.* Reading, MA: Addison-Wesley.

———. S. Wieder., and R. Simons. 1998. *The child with special needs.* Reading, MA: Addison-Wesley.

Haldy, M., and L. Haack. 1995. *Making it easy.* San Antonio: Therapy Skill Builders.

Hanft, B., and P. Place. 1996. *The consulting therapist.* San Antonio: Therapy Skill Builders.

Hersch, F. 2003. *Soothing the senses.* Las Vegas: Sensory Resources. Compact disk.

Hickman, L., and R. Hutchins. 2002. *Seeing clearly.* 2d ed. Las Vegas: Sensory Resources.

Kashman, N. and J. Mora. 2005. *The sensory connection: An OT and SLP team approach.* Las Vegas: Sensory Resources.

Koomar, J., S. Szklut, and S. Cermak. 2004. *Making sense of sensory integration.* 2d ed. Las Vegas: Sensory Resources. Compact disk.

Kranowitz, C. S. 1995. *101 activities for kids in tight spaces.* New York: St. Martin's Griffin.

———. 2001. *The out-of-sync child.* 90 min. Las Vegas: Sensory Resources. Videocassette.

———. 2002. *Getting kids in sync.* 30 min. Las Vegas: Sensory Resources. Videocassette.

———. 2003. *The out-of-sync child has fun.* New York: Perigee.

———. 2004. *The Goodenoughs get in sync: An introduction to sensory processing disorder and sensory integration.* Las Vegas: Sensory Resources.

———. 2005. *The out-of-sync child: Recognizing and coping with sensory processing disorder.* 2d ed. New York: Perigee.

Lande, A., B. Wiz, and L. Hickman. 1999. *Songames for sensory integration.* 2d ed. Las Vegas: Sensory Resources. Compact disk and booklet.

MaBoAubLo, and B. Sher. 2005. *28 instant songames.* 3d ed. Las Vegas: Sensory Resources. Compact disk and booklet.

Morris, S. E. 2002. *Marvelous mouth music.* 2d ed. Las Vegas: Sensory Resources. Compact disk and booklet.

Renke, L. 2005. *I like birthdays…it's the parties I'm not sure about!* Las Vegas: Sensory Resources.

Richter, E., P. Oetter, and S. Frick. 1993. *MORE: Integrating the mouth with sensory and postural functions.* Hugo, MN: PDP Press.

Seiderman, A. S., and S. E. Marcus. 1991. *20/20 is not enough: The new world of vision.* New York: Fawcett Crest.

Silver, M.D., L. B. 1992. *The misunderstood child: A guide for parents of children with learning disabilities.* 3d ed. Blue Ridge Summit, PA: TAB Books.

———. 1993. *Dr. Larry Silver's advice to parents on ADHD.* 2d ed. New York: Three Rivers Press.

Szklut, S., S. Cermak, and A. Henderson. 1995. *Learning disabilities.* In *Neurological rehabilitation.* 3d ed. edited by D. Umphred (New York: C. V. Mosby).

Szklut, S., and C. S. Kranowitz. 2005. *Teachers ask about sensory integration.* Las Vegas: Sensory Resources. Compact disk.

Taylor, K. F., C. McDonald, and A. Lande. 2002. *Danceland.* 2d ed. Las Vegas: Sensory Resources. Compact disk and booklet.

Trott, M. C., M. Laurel, and S. L. Windeck. 1993. *SenseAbilities: Understanding sensory integration.* San Antonio: Therapy Skill Builders.

Vail, P. L. 1996. *Words fail me: How language works and what happens when it doesn't.* Rosemont, NJ: Modern Learning Press.

Whalen, C. 2005. *Songs for sensational kids. vol. 1: The wiggly scarecrow.* Mill Creek, WA: Lava Falls Publishing. Compact disk. (All proceeds benefit The Kid Foundation for sensory processing disorder research and awareness).

Williams, M. S., and S. Shellenberger. 1992. *Introduction to how does your engine run? The alert program for self-regulation.* Albuquerque: Therapy Works.

———. 1994. *How does your engine run? A leader's guide to the alert program for self-regulation.* Albuquerque: Therapy Works.

Yack, E.; S. Sutton, and P. Aquilla. 2003. *Building bridges through sensory integration.* 2d ed. Las Vegas: Sensory Resources.